IN FACT

IN FACT

By

JOHN CIARDI

RUTGERS UNIVERSITY PRESS

NEW BRUNSWICK, NEW JERSEY

ACKNOWLEDGEMENTS

Some of these poems originally appeared in *Saturday Review*, copyright 1962, and in *Poetry*, copyright 1962.

TO *Father William*

who has grown old standing me
on my head, I pause in the act
of growing no younger, to offer
these lines ever fondly.

CONTENTS

SELECTIVITY   3

COME MORNING   4

MY TRIBE   5

A FABLE OF SURVIVAL   6

ON BEING SURE AND OF WHAT   8

THEIR EYES WATCHING   9

ORDERS   10

MISS OLIVIA BRANTON   12

POETRY   14

IN PITY AS WE KISS AND LIE   15

NOTHING WOULD COME OF THIS   16

DEATH'S THE CLASSIC LOOK   17

CREDIBILITY   18

4:00 A.M. ON THE TERRACE   19

VODKA   20

FAST AS YOU CAN COUNT TO TEN   21

RETURNING HOME   22

SATURDAY   23

EGGS   24

EVERYTIME YOU ARE SLEEPING AND I   25

BY THE SEA   26

BIRD WATCHING   28

IF YOU REALLY FEEL YOU   29

DAWN OF THE SPACE AGE   30

A MISSOURI FABLE   31

TEMPTED AT THE ALGONQUIN BY SUCH A CHOICE   32

ORATION   33

QUESTION   34

THE MESSAGE-BEARER   35

IN PAUL'S ROOM   36

AS I WOULD WISH YOU BIRDS   37

HERITAGE   39

WHEN I AM NOT DEAD   40

THE TRAGEDY-MAKER   42

ARE WE THROUGH TALKING, I HOPE?   44

I'M NO GOOD FOR YOU   45

THE DAYS NO WOLF COMES THERE ARE NO WOLVES   47

EPITAPH FOR GEORGE   48

IN MY FATHER'S HOUSE THERE ARE A FEW MANSIONS, ETC.   49

CLOSE-OUT   50

ENGLISH A   51

DOWN NARROW STAIRS FROM A THIN EYE   52

ONE FOR REXROTH   54

OF THE KINGDOM   55

ONE JAY AT A TIME   56

CONSUMER RESEARCH   57

SUBURBAN HOMECOMING   58

SOMETIMES RUNNING   59

SONNET   60

viii

TO A PLATFORM FULL OF COMMUTERS   61

MISS ASPIC   62

IN SOME DOUBT BUT WILLINGLY   64

COUNTING ON FLOWERS   65

LETTER TO A WRONG CHILD   66

IN FACT

SELECTIVITY

Now mist takes the hemlocks and nothing
stirs. This is a gray-green and a
glassy thing and nothing stirs. A plane
to or from Newark burrs down idling on
its flaps or grinds full-rich up its
airy grade, and I hear it. Mrs. Levy calls
her kids and I hear her. A train eight
blocks away rolls and I hear it. And
tire sounds. And a car door closing
dully. And a whole helluva caterwaul
when Richard hits Benn again and Benn does
stir. He comes running. And I hear it.
And then the phone rings and, carefully,
I do not hear it. I am listening selectively.

COME MORNING

A young cock in his plebe strut
mounts the rail-fence to some
reviewing stand he has in mind
and practices commanding all those
dim regiments eastward.
                    Not bad, boy!
Not quite full-toned, but willing.
You'll make it yet!
                    But suddenly
the damned Daddy-Colonel of them
all unfurls above our shavetail
like a flaming umbrella in a high
wind, and that's all brother! Our
lad's mustered out and running like
any civilian with hot hell on his tail.

Go it, boy! Old Jab-and-Spur has
blood in mind!
                    Till here comes
the Colonel back again strutting
posh as the dream of horse-guards,
sets himself in place like Victoria's
best bustle, and, sucking a sky in,
lets go with the right high hot sound
for it, and makes it official. It's
morning!

MY TRIBE

Everyone in my tribe hates
everyone in your tribe.

Every girl in my tribe wants to
be there when we bring in anyone
from your tribe. Our girls save faggots
in their hope chests for you.

Every boy in my tribe has a peg
from which to hang the scalp of
anyone in your tribe. Our boys
hone knives in their dreams of you.

Everyone in my tribe is proud of
our boys and their dreams, of our
girls and their trousseaus. Our lives
have dear goals across which we

shall all finally kick all of your
heads. We are united.

A FABLE OF SURVIVAL

One of my neighbors began digging himself
an air-raid shelter week-ends. He had religion:
eight hours Saturdays, eight Sundays, a cubic yard
a day, starting in March. By mid-August,
even though, by then, he needed rigging
to hoist the dirt, he made two yards a sweat.
On the long Labor Day Weekend he made seven
with a clever bucket and pulley and his wife.
I guessed she had read Noah, too. By October
they had their hole dug twelve by twelve by fourteen
and thought it wouldn't do, but stopped for winter.

We had them in for cocktails to celebrate.
No strings attached. I pledged him in good bourbon
I wouldn't crowd in if the skies let go.
But what, I asked, if it happened before the thaw?
Or if his hole wasn't deep down enough.
How deep *was* deep enough? Suppose next Fall
he had it twenty-four by twelve by fourteen
and guessed it wouldn't do and had to wait
another winter, and it happened then,
with his hole still open? Wouldn't it be simpler
to take a boat to China and dig from there?

He took my drinks but wouldn't take my jokes.
A man can't dig that long unless he's preaching
inside himself at every shovel-full.
He had a sermon to the cubic yard.
And data, blueprints, catalogs, specifications.
He couldn't have sounded more in Godly earnest—
or grander, or more memorized, or more saved—
had he been selling cigarettes on TV.
He had the Truth. He had, by God, the Truth.

I told him we were rival denominations.
That he swore by the shovel and I by bourbon.
He did point out that bourbon had first to be saved.
But he wasn't joking. Only being polite.
He was so saved he could be tolerant.

It was his wife took me aside and scolded.
"Good heavens," I told her—we had been friends once,
before survival—"don't tell me you're bitten, too?
If you want sermons, I can preach you one:
that mind's the only shelter left—whatever
shelter there is in that—though even that's
harder to come by than a hole in the ground,
and won't be shoveled at as clean as dirt."

I had a lot to say—or bourbon did—
of how I'd rather take it on the roof.
I said I had a case stashed by the hatch
and the ice-bucket on alert. I hadn't,
but I liked the notion better as I said it.
Then I was off on statistics. I invented
enough to feed the press for seven months.
She shook her head. *"I'll* join you on the roof.
But *look* at him! He's twenty good pounds younger.
Tough as nails. And, brother, he's got *fervor!"*

That's when I understood about survival.

ON BEING SURE AND OF WHAT

Salmon are very sure
of something. They endure
the eating sea, the falling
river and its hauling
edges of nets and spears,
and otters, too, and bears.
Then when at last they win
to the still waters in
the rock-pools of the sky
they spend their eggs and die.
What saint flings harder at
his martyrdom? Our cat
finishing the can
that we began
completes the commentary.
Here ends this bestiary.

THEIR EYES WATCHING

Miguel Dominguin, Don Miguel, the Matador
asked himself why men enter the arena
and found his answer in women, in the
presence of women. "If there were no
women there, no man would face the
bulls. At least I should not."

Think of yourself in the tiers of
their lives—can you?—in the way
their breath stops at the moment
of truth. Is it an arena or a cave-
mouth they sit in to watch you?
sending you to your most encounter

with that silence you walk up to
inside yourself? feeling their eyes?
feeling the sperm-pump of danger
drive you full at the touch of
their eyes in you?—You, *Torero,*
your body of dangerous graces!

ORDERS

Gulls in Wyoming, Utah, follow the plows,
picking the small jet lives from the turned furrows.

It half unfastens nature, their being there
a mile up and a thousand in from the sea.

In Gloucester, yes. In Manilla, Capetown, Dover—
by all the salt-shot names of the edges,

and slid beyond the edges, following, wide
and easy on the wind, the turned wakes, there—

at home where all mind trespasses and prays
and the impossible is a habitat—

there a man can answer with a psalm
from true-salt the blue dream a gull is.

But these landlubbers, half-hen and half-buzzard,
picking black lice out of the desert's pores—

call these things gulls? I call them bleached crows!
—Or did. Until I saw the sea still leaving,

first in Red Desert country, then in Salt Lake.
It must be salt deceives them from themselves:

somehow they smell it but can't find the water.
How could they guess at years-ago by millions?

I think they're queerly lost by a right instinct.
Or else they're only waiting, their instinct sound,

to be on hand when the next ocean starts here.
I wish they'd go to sea where they belong

and let the hawks and buzzards have the desert
in their own terms, as if it meant to last.

And then again I'm glad they're queerly home:
their presence teaches possibility

another range. And every man a moral:
put wings to a stomach and all the world is reached.

MISS OLIVIA BRANTON

I remember Miss Olivia Branton, which
wasn't her name, but let that go. She was
the dumbest high-school teacher I ever
felt superior to, which I did instantly.
I don't think she had even read the books
she asked us to read. And she certainly
had never read anything else. Not that I
objected to her making a living. Everyone
has to one way or another. But why
couldn't she have been an honest char-
woman? Certainly she could have learned
to wring out a mop with a little practice,
which would have been a damned sight
better than saying "aren't I" and "like I
say" and "it's very unique" and "I'm truly
enthused" to, mind you, an English class.

She was so dumb that once I discovered
she simply did not understand how insulting
my papers were, I began to feel protective
about her. She thought I was some damned
kind of genius, poor clod. She was especially
a push-over for Greek mythology, and my God,
even when I wrote that Leda was a goose-girl
that pulled a feather from a gander's tail and,
using it as a magic wand, changed herself into a
narcissus, she—Miss Olivia Branton, that is—
wrote: "Another splendid example of the appeal
your imagination has for wide reading, and
beautifully expressed, like always. You will go
far."—I mean, my God, there comes a time when
you have to love the helpless just because they

are helpless, than which no one more uniquely was.
I didn't even have sex-fantasies about Miss Olivia
Branton, and those days I could have had sex-
fantasies about a female totem-pole if it had a
skirt on it. Half the time when I was called to
recite, I had to bend over the desk nearly-double
to keep from being obvious. But any bulge I stood
up with in her class was pure and detached plain
overflowing joy-juices. Not that Miss Branton was
bad-looking. She was all right in a confused-dolly
sort of way, but she was so lost that her own
husband (had she had one) would have felt like a
rapist if he so much as kissed her goodbye in the
doorway after breakfast. She was so helpless and
dumb I kept feeling like everybody's father (which
is a hell of a sex) whenever she opened her mouth and
let another moth flutter out of her cocoon brain.

And that, I guess, is why I fell in love with her,
though it was more nearly the way you love your
baby-sister, if you have one. I didn't have any
baby-sisters. Not aside from Miss Olivia Branton.
I ran her errands, and washed her blackboards, and
explained *The Decline of the West* to her (I had a
Spengler jag then) which she didn't have a dream
of understanding how much I misunderstood. She
thought it was wonderful to know a damn genius even
if she couldn't tell the difference between a genius
and a McCormick spreader with a vocabulary attachment,
or, as a matter of fact, just because she couldn't
tell the difference, and neither could I. I loved her
about twice as purely as you could imagine and with no
sex-fantasies, and when she left town I was very adult
about saying goodbye, but when I got home I cried.

POETRY

Whether or not you like it is not my
business/whether or not you can take
it is, finally, yours/whether or not
it makes any difference to you it does
make its own, whether or not you see it.

Whether or not you see it is not your
business alone/whether or not it tells
you the difference between yourself and
busyness, it does tell whether or not.

IN PITY AS WE KISS AND LIE

Softly wrong, we lie and kiss,
heart to heart and thigh to thigh.
Like man and woman. As if this
were how and who and when and why.

Some two in the time of man
and woman found it sweet
to trade what such half-bodies can
that both be made complete.

Some two in a place that was
hardly right but softly true
found themselves and founded us—
he to her and I to you.

Softly wrong and hardly right,
heart to heart and thigh to thigh,
in each others arms tonight
we lie and kiss and kiss and lie.

If he by her and I by you,
like man and woman, now and then
find each other softly true—
what of how, who, why, and when?

Till hardly wrong, as mercy is—
when and how and who and why—
softly right we lie and kiss
in pity as we kiss and lie.

NOTHING WOULD COME OF THIS

Nothing would come of this
night I sat to. "This is the
night you died," I kept saying
to you, thinking I might make
the night speak its difference
from all others. It said, and I
listened: frog-burr, traffic-buzz,
cricket-rub, but no sound of
whatever your dying must mean to
make and remember I loved you
and that nothing would come of
it. It was a night, and no poem
in it to say if from all nights.
"Damn poetry," I said and took to
vodka-and-tonic and you stayed
dead to the end of the bottle and
I threw it away and it made some
sound, technically, but the cold
clinic of fact aside, none in any
meaning that could say: "I loved you
and no sound will come of it now."

DEATH'S THE CLASSIC LOOK

Death's the classic look. It goes
down stoneworks carved with Latin Prose
and Poetry. And scholar's Greek
that no one now can really speak,
though it's all guessed at. The long view
contains bits of Etruscan, too,
(as guessed at as the Greek is, but
no one yet has figured out
more than a first few words, and those
the names for fish, bird, water, rose
painted beside the painting of
what a dead man kept to love
inside his tomb). In back of that
the view runs desert-rimmed and flat
past writings that were things, not words:
roses, water, fish, and birds.
The thing before the letters came,
the name before there was a name.
And back of things themselves? Who knows?
Jungle spells it as it grows
where the damp among the shoots
waterlogs the classic roots,
and the skulls and bones of things
last half as long as a bird sings,
as a fish swims, as a rose fills,
opens, lets out its breath, and spills
into the sockets where things crawl,
and death looks like no look at all.

CREDIBILITY

Who could believe an ant in theory?
a giraffe in blueprint?
Ten thousand doctors of what's possible
could reason half the jungle out of being.
I speak of love, and something more,
to say we are the thing that proves itself
not against reason, but impossibly true,
and therefore to teach reason reason.

4:00 A.M. ON THE TERRACE

I should—but anyone can and
therefore why?—go to bed. I
should get more sleep. I should
be rested when I go tomorrow to
do what anyone can—and bring
it home. I should think more of
my health. I should keep regular
hours as anyone can.

                    But where,
tomorrow, will this night be full
of frog-beep and bug-Morse among
these stars that no one might
time-travel if I should not and
regularly never bring home?

VODKA

Vodka, I hope you will note, is
upwind from all other essences.
Drink it all night and all day
and your aunt's minister could
not track you to perdition, not
even with his nose for it. Vodka
has no breath. Call it the dead-
man's drink. But praise it. As
long as he can stand, a vodka-
drinker is sober, and when he
falls down he is merely sleepy.
Like poetry, vodka informs anything with which it is diluted,
and like poetry, alas, it must be
diluted. Only a Russian can take
it straight, and only after long
conditioning, and just see what
seems to be coming of that!

FAST AS YOU CAN COUNT TO TEN

Fast as you can count to ten
commandments, I would count to
twenty forgivenesses, could I
think which twenty, and till I
can, let me offer all and without number and beg for myself,
if you please, your used mercies.

RETURNING HOME

I want to tell you a
gentlest thing. Like light
to you. Like old faces
being fed a good memory
from inside themselves.
Like eyes that do not
watch but slowly meet
across a room in which
everyone is, and no one
need hurry to what he is
sure of. I want to say
before we run out of
rooms and everyone
that I am slowest,
surest, gentlest, too,
across whatever room
I look at you.

SATURDAY

The power-mown morning of this spang
green world we have moved to opens roaring
from all house-held lawns. Daddy's home
up and down all the street, his growlers
spinning the other side of the thickets
to right and left and over the hedges
I hear him up and down at his sentry-
go that this world may stay trim and
told in its duty loudly.

                    So summoned
I wake and dutifully do my own bright
blurrer to its loud life and up and down
over my grasses make the noise of this
place in straight rows from thicket to
thicket and between the hedges while
from the tree-fort my sly gunners sight,
their arms shouting commands I can
glimpse but not hear, mowing me down
or suddenly pointing upward to blast a
plane from anywhere in its last traffic-
pattern to Newark, and then lunch.

EGGS

The egg a chick pokes its head out of
is a process of nature. The egg I
bit by bit got my head out of was a
process of propriety.
                There are great
chemistries to be recorded of the
natural egg. Of these confections in
which we systematically embalm the
young, there is to be said only that
they are generally too sweet, that
in hot weather they get sticky, and
that they are all hell to fertilize.

EVERYTIME YOU ARE SLEEPING AND I

Everytime you are sleeping and I
am not I like to watch your far
breathing wakefully counting this
and far nights tenderly dark with
thoughts closely and farther yet
nights when you will not be closely
thus thought of in any way nor I

BY THE SEA

If you must drag Heaven to bed,
note this about Zeus, darling,
if he will do as a sample God—
that though he got around to
the daughters of earth, there
was no love in his going. All
those swan-dives, bull-lunges,
and showers of gold were no more
than vacation trips from the
sky that was too long even
for him who was as long as it.
Or exactly because he was as
long as it, being different from
it only in that he knew how long
he was.

But being that—do you
see?—timeless and knowing he
was, how *could* he love? What
could hurry him to love? He
could think centuries on each
dabble into the flesh, foresee
it, create it, and then let it
happen (or not) in the same
reverie as his sky changing
from one distance to another.

Suppose I had my choice of
whatever centuries before I
need think of beginning to love
you, what difference could it
make if I came to you before or

after that mountain chain or this
ocean came and went?

               It is because
I am no Zeus (whatever)—do you
still follow?—that I hurry this
time of mole-hills to grab for
other and, I will believe, better
skies than all his and forever as
soon as you will let them be.

BIRD WATCHING

Everytime we put crumbs out and sunflower
seeds something comes. Most often sparrows.
Frequently a jay. Now and then a junco or
a cardinal. And once—immediately and never
again, but as commonly as any miracle while it
is happening, and then instantly incredible forever—the tiniest (was it?) yellow warbler
as nearly as I could thumb through the bird
book for it, or was it an escaped canary? or
simply the one impossible bright bird that is
always there during a miracle, and then never?

I, certainly, do not know all that comes to us
at times. A bird is a bird as long as it is
there. Then it is a miracle our crumbs and
sunflower seeds caught and let go. Is there
a book to look through for the identity
of a miracle? No bird that is there is
miracle enough. Every bird that has been is
entirely one. And if some miracles are rarer
than others, every incredible bird has crumbs
and seeds in common with every other. Let there
be bread and seed in time: all else will follow.

IF YOU REALLY FEEL YOU

If you really feel you owe it to the human
race, to yourself, or to your idea of the
relationship you are trying to establish
between yourself and it, then, whatever it is,
do it. Whatever else you do, for whatever
other reason, is certainly aside from whatever
the point really is, if you feel you.

DAWN OF THE SPACE AGE

First a monkey, then a man.
Just the way the world began.

A MISSOURI FABLE

A man named Finchley once
without thinking much about
it broke into the premises of
Mr. Billy Jo Trant of these
parts, by which felonious
entry he meant to separate
Mr. Billy Jo from various
properties, but stepping on
a noise without thinking
enough about it woke Mr.
Billy Jo who took in hand a
Colt .45 and, improvising the
order of his rebuttal, fired
three times in an entirely
accurate way and then said
"Hands up!" without thinking
that the man named Finchley
once was not listening as
carefully as he might have
had Mr. Billy Jo thought to
disagree with him in a
slightly different order.

Moral: commit yourself to
another man's premises and
you may, in logic, have to
accept his conclusion.

TEMPTED AT THE ALGONQUIN BY SUCH A CHOICE

Tempted at the Algonquin by such a choice
fluff as enters, to be sure, every memoir,
I will not immediately have that drink too
many but willfully trade signals until the
Director and the Producer and the Writer drink
up, shake hands around, and leave, leaving
Her. It is, of course, five o'clock and in
another hour it will be six and so from hour
to hour we ripe and ripe, I spacing my drinks
soberfully among such spas as flesh leads
her to nibbling little things from trays
that are passed by the same waiter who keeps
changing the color of his sleeve from red to
green to blue to purple-with-a-gold stripe till
here we are somewhere high in, probably, the
Sheraton-Plaza and what she says as we uncoil
and she heads for the shower in elegant rondure
dimpled is, "What happened to dinner?" and as
I pick up the telephone, "I'll drink mine, baby."

ORATION

The day I can tear up my pass-
port and take out citizenship in
the human race—which I would
gladly the cries of Treason face—
that day I will buy ice-cream
for all the kids in every color and
flavor, and butterflies for every
rose and bud, and hamburger for
little silver piranhe in their lost
Amazon seeking, that they be fed,
and gladly for the lion stalking
his gold plains what saints will
offer of themselves to him, and
for the unknown soldiery its radiant
pension, and gladly as many shares
of Consolidated Everything as I
can get margin for and even and
beyond treason gladly bourbon
for those same Senators crying
whose flags I will gladly waive.

QUESTION

Of all the
people who
go swimming
in mirages
how many do
you suppose
actually
manage to
get wet?

I ask this
drowningly
in no water,
thinking of
you—and you—
splashlessly
in all ocean.

THE MESSAGE-BEARER

She stormed the restaurant
flapping like one of her own
pamphlets in the wind she made
of herself. "Have you heard?"
she cried, lifting her face into
that wind, and the pamphlets
flew from her hands like birds.
"There is no more death!" And a
bird dropped at each plate, its
wings stamped LIFE ETERNAL. "Have
you heard?" she sang and the birds
flew from her.
        It was a hot day
and, God, how she stank.
           The head-
waiter tried to ease her out,
but this gal was no man's easement.
She stank firm in her zeal. She had
the word and was not leaving without
our souls.
        Until the cop took her
by the elbow. "C'mon, sister." And
they stood on the sidewalk by the
plate-glass: the cop, the savior,
and the headwaiter till the wagon
rolled up and the cop put her in
and the head-waiter came back
shaking his head. "Bellevue,"
he said and began picking up the
dead birds. "Please excuse it."
And a bus-boy appeared with an
atomizer and did delicately spray.

IN PAUL'S ROOM

This is Paul whose habits are
all he has to die of. He
has survived a shooting war,
an auto wreck, two wives, and three
collapses into Bellevue.
Tell me, bottle, tell me true:
do you drink him? does he drink you?

When Paul has seen his final Thing,
twitched his final twitch, and lies
very dead, what radiant wing
will descend out of the skies
to the cold still of his brain
that his rotted soul again
stretch and lift? When Paul has lain

in statistics and a sigh,
tell me bottle, tell me true,
will you lift his soul on high
for all those years he lifted you?
Paul is here but Paul is dead.
There is no one in his head.
All that was Paul has been shed.

I remember, you do not,
what was Paul a thirst ago.
How do good men go to rot?
Is that something I could know?
If I drank you for a clue,
tell me, bottle, tell me true:
could I taste the Paul in you?

AS I WOULD WISH YOU BIRDS

Today—because I must not lie to you—
there are no birds but such as I wish
for. There is only my wish to wish you
birds. Catbirds with spatula tails up
jaunty. Jays, gawky as dressed-up toughs.
Humming birds, their toy engines going.
Turkeys with Savanarola heads. Bitchy
Peacocks. The rabble of Hens in their
stinking harems—these three (and
Ostriches and Dodos) a sadness to think
about. But then Gulls—ultimate bird
everywhere everything pure wing and wind
are, there over every strut, flutter, cheep,
coo. At Dover over the pigeon-cliffs.
At Boston over the sparrows. Off tropics
where the lyre-tails and the green-
iridescent heads flash. And gone again.

You never see Gulls in aviaries. Gulls are
distance. Who can put distance in a cage?

Today—and I could never lie to you—
there is no distance equal to what I wish
for. There is only my wish to wish you
a distance full of birds, a thronged air
lifting above us far, lifting us, the sun
bursting in cloud chambers, a choir there
pouring light years of song, its wings
flashing. See this with me. Close your eyes
and see what air can do with more birds in it
than anything but imagination can put there.
There are not enough birds in the eyes we

37

open. There are too many hens, turkeys, and
that peacock seen always on someone else's
lawn, the air above it wasted unused, songless.
Birds cannot be seen in fact. Not enough
of them at once, not now nor any day. But think
with me what might be, but close your eyes and see.

HERITAGE

"Never trust the arithmetic of the poor," my
father said. "Except for that business of going forth and multiplying what the rich will
lovingly divide, the poor are abacuses without beads. They can and do finger their own
wires, but you have to have something to put
over before you can be sure of the difference
between addition and subtraction." So said my
old father in the act of leaving me no estate
except, maybe, his sense of humor, if there is
anything to be said well for the prospects of
a comedian without the price of a joke-book.

WHEN I AM NOT DEAD

When I am not dead I
see and can remember
everything. I am able
and well-feasted. I
can go to anything
for it to happen, or
wait for it to come.
I know your name deep
as you wait to know
it. I am there wait-
ing and being your
name. I can say sun
and the shadow of all
names in it. I can
count fishes by rings
on a ripple. I love
and am instantly be-
lievable and can wait
for every instant I
am
    and then I do die
(the telephone rings,
a car stops, a calend-
ar clicks into an air-
plane and fastens its
seat-belt, the host-
ess smiles, I talk to
salesmen and get off)
and do not know I have
died and do not know
even that I am wait-
ing

until instantly
sometimes I am again
not dead and I see and
can remember every-
thing I am, and your
name, and sun, and our
shadow in it and that
I was always (and did
not know it) waiting.

THE TRAGEDY-MAKER

Everything you/I/we do in the natural course
she did on tightropes over abysses. Any man/
woman/child, God knows, risks falling. She
made sure of it. Look through your town for
the man most likely to put his head into the
oven: she married him, prodded him into having
six kids before he did take the gas-pipe, and
nearly died of each of them. She fell and
broke her hip when she was five months gone
to the first, but had it. With the second it
was pneumonia, but she had it. With the third
it was second degree burns from the oil heater,
but she had it. She fell downstairs with the
fifth, but she had it. The fourth and sixth
almost killed her with no outside assistance,
but she had them—the sixth in time to nurse
at its father's funeral. Then she killed herself for twenty years keeping them fed and
keeping them from killing themselves and one
another, and just keeping them. One way or
another, keeping them. Until she began to
lose them one by one. One got drafted and
killed in training at Fort Bragg (he went on
maneuvers and bedded down in the dark on what
turned out to be a road) and she buried him and
one took a Fourth of July weekend around a curve
too fast and she buried him and one just walked
away and never looked back and she couldn't
bury him and wept maybe because he spoiled her
collection and one took the ancestral gas-pipe
and there of course she was on familiar ground
(in which she buried him) and one—he was a

cop—shook down the wrong Sicilian and they
boxed them separately without being entirely
sure of some of the pieces and she buried hers,
and the last one took a baseball bat to a girl
lovingly and got himself buried alive in State
storage and there was another to spoil her collection until finally morning by morning she
came to one day dimmer than all and could not
wake to it and they buried her and from somewhere a wreath came saying *Mother* and she lay
there, just she and the wreath that no one
came with, not looking at one another, and
then they buried her and whatever it was she
was she finally was not, poor bird, poor husk,
poor sufferer at everything, and at last done.

ARE WE THROUGH TALKING, I HOPE?

Why do I have to make
sense? What sense is
there to make unless
our senses make it? I
don't want to make
sense. I want sensibly
to make you because any
thing else is nonsense
and what sense is there
in that?

I'M NO GOOD FOR YOU

I'm no good for you and you'
re no good for me, we'
re no good for this that or
anything unless, even at
the risk of being bump-
tious, we let our skins be
skins and our bellies be
bellies and our lips be for
   giving.

A ghost in the sun so hairy
with light he seems to be a
fire as he comes, seems to be
lanced with rays and aureoled
and with birds mating in and
out of him as he comes, seems to
be naked as light on the dew on the
   grasses,

to be seen through more shining,
to redouble all first green-
light, seems to be walking in
your eyes and my eyes to a
blessing in both of us, seems to be
easily the kindliest and most
   radiant

thought we have of our
selves here naked in our
first green (if we can be for
giving) seems to be our

most sun-up of everything.
And he comes. That ghost (if
rarely) does (now) entirely
    come.

THE DAYS NO WOLF COMES THERE ARE NO WOLVES

The days no wolf comes there are
lawns and breezeways: the 9:10
goes in: the 5:07 comes out: the car
dutch-ovens all day at the station, then
opens to oak-and-maple air
down the nice street the big white
houses stand their century to. Just past
the first town, the second: green-bright
and new: the lawns bigger, barer, caste-
marked by cedar-splits round the pools
to which no wolf comes: not in the memory
of all our wives, our good schools,
the landscaped neighbors we see
tinkling ice-cubes, patio'd in the sun.
The days no wolf comes there are none.

EPITAPH FOR GEORGE

It takes some genius to drown in
dew but since George would not
go near any water more than film-
deep, and to the extent that we
must all metaphorically drown in
something, there was, by a simple
process of elimination, nothing
else for him to do, and he did it.

IN MY FATHER'S HOUSE THERE ARE A FEW MANSIONS, MORE HOVELS, AND PROBABLY EVEN MORE RANCH-HOUSES

Some men live in, say, houses and some
in their own monuments. The poor live in
what they can get; the rich, in what they
can imagine of themselves; the clerks, in
what they are told to imagine through the
picture windows.

Given the money for it,
a man can begin to buy whatever it is that
furnishes his imagination. Given no money,
he is left to live without the furniture
for his own attitudes. Given some—more
or less—money, a man fits his attitudes
to the furniture he is allowed to buy with
what he is given.

Given a picture-window,
citizen, make sure it looks out onto something. Which is also to say, out from
something, preferably, I suggest, a Self.

CLOSE-OUT

After 7 days of no-calory food and
with only a skim-world left to rest
on, there came utter lightlessness
bursting, a change of vowels, and
then nothing, infinitely, to say.

ENGLISH A

No paraphrase does
between understanding
and understanding.

You are either
that noun beyond
qualification into

whose round fact
I pass unparsed
and into whose eyes

I speak idioms
beyond construction;
or else get up,

fasten your suffixes
and your hyphenations,
buckle your articles,

spray modifiers
and moods
behind your ears

and take the whole
developed discourse
of your thighs to

any damned grammarian
you whatsoever
wish. Period.

51

DOWN NARROW STAIRS FROM A THIN EYE

"If all example is from nature," I thought as I left the apartment of a (particularly) poet, "not all of nature can be imagined to exist in form for convenient reference." He must, my thought ran on, answer to some parable from if not yet quite in nature, but what? So it began:

"Were there," I thought, "in those furry waves of compulsion lemmings form down from their hill-boroughs in their gross seizure to the sea, some particular fur-piece entirely intoxicated by its presence in the race of that tide, yet conditioned to an even more consuming—to an ultimate—dread of salt water, I could (had it a name) cite it in a single neat word as nature's ready equivalence, and I should not need then detail its first far sniff of that sea: how, within one madness, it would wake to find itself raked by another, swept forward within a compulsion to the unbearable: what agonies would contend in it to the wetting of a first toe: and how it would turn then from one sea to be overborne by another: how it would panic backward on that furry-brown tidal conveyor-belt moving forward faster than even panic could outdo itself backward—and lose: until there was nothing left but the one sea in which it frothed and fought another: and how, clenched finally into a spasm like *rigor mortis,* it would float there among particles, lacking all particularity." Nature has specified no such example. Its existence, therefore, may be cited among the uses of the imagination, but with all the inconveniences of having to shape it from inventory, at the risk of boring that suicide who grabs his deaths in gluttonous gulps of his own monologue; and on the other hand of going completely over the head of that exemplar who is navigating his conveyor-belt to incorporated immortalities and who will (quote) be damned if he knows what you're talking about and even (quote) more so if he doesn't. As for that poet from whose apartment I was coming, I have just recalled that I do not know any such person except to go away from and gladly.

ONE FOR REXROTH

I know a man in San Francisco
with a round head, glassy eyes,
a terrier hair-cut, and a voice
like gravel down a chute. Holy
Hollywood would sooner submit to
mentality than let him be filmed
kissing the American girl. All
the same he gets around, thank
you. He is my friend. A good
poet. And a man of love and
learning. I do not imply that he
is perfect. I do say that he
exceeds the language of which
all your saleable images are
compounded/that the eyes to
which he is visible have
publicly offended/and that
they must be plucked out before
the kingdom may be wholly to the blind.

OF THE KINGDOM

If you will let people be wrong,
most of whatever love is
may begin. Justice will hang
all of us yet. Waft mercies
the guilty may walk on when
truth grows absolute. The trees
from which we shall dangle then
are everywhere. And since
not all trees can be cut,
all men may hang. But once
let love in, mercy out, ah, then
a bird song may defend us,
a mote—can you dream it?—heal!

ONE JAY AT A TIME

I have never seen a
generalized blue jay.
I have never heard a
specific one utter a
denial. Blue jays are
one at a time and they
are always screamers
of an assertion. Look
at that stiff dandy on
the sill-box. YES! YES!
YES! he screams forever
on a launching pad in-
side himself. I AM! I AM!
I AM! AND HERE I GO!

CONSUMER RESEARCH

I am no customer whatever for most of those most
popular products on which the economy has, you may
say, flourished. I do not bowl, nor drink coca-
cola, nor go to the movies. It is at least twenty
years since I thought about a circus, or a rodeo,
or a prize fight, or a ball game. Last year (I have
read) we produced 300 million 45 rpm recordings not
one of which I bought. And though I have been a
supporting member of National Distillers and of
Ligget and Myers' probably carcinogenic weeds, I have
seldom willingly voted for either of those parties
that keep carrying elections in spite of me. I do
not, certainly, buy sports equipment. And though I
could once shave eighty on the course (with a little
winking) I have not shot as many as five rounds in
ten years. I am sometimes, in fact, bewildered by the
number of markets that flourish without even my
regrets. But if you are even remotely in inventory
(baby) I am just that plunger who will go into hock
up to his teeth and eyebrows to stock-pile You.

SUBURBAN HOMECOMING

As far as most of what you call people, my darling, are
concerned, I don't care who or what gets into the phone. I
am not home and not expected and I even, considerably,
   doubt I live here.

I mean this town and its everlasting katzenjammer whenever whoever dials again, is going to hell, or to some other
perpetual buffet, in a wheelbarrowful of bad martinis: and
   you, my

legal sweet, forever in the act of putting your hat on
as I come in the door to be told I have exactly five—
or, on good days, ten—minutes to change in because here we
   go

again to some collection of never-quite-the-same-but-
always-no-different faces; you, my moth-brained flutter
from bright cup to cup, no matter what nothing is in them;
   you, my own

brand-named, laboratory-tested, fair-trade-priced, wedded
(as advertised in *Life*) feather-duster, may go jump into
twenty fathoms of Advice to the Lovelorn and pull it in after
   you—

but I have not arrived, am not it, the phone did not ring
and was not answered, we have not really, I believe, met, and
if we do and if I stay to be (I doubt it) introduced, I'm still
   not going.

SOMETIMES RUNNING

Sometimes running
to yes nothing and
too fast to look
where and at what
I stand and there
are trees sunning
themselves long a
brook going and
jays and jewelry
in all leafages
because I pause.

SONNET

"What has to happen," said the old man
in a voice that would do for most mercy—
"what has to happen is so certainly already
on its way to being nothing that nothing can
change us now. It is not change this dead pan
face of the day needs for eyes, but more nearly
a recollection. I cannot say it exactly.
It is a matter of feeling. But if you needed an
eye to see with, could you find it here?
The eyes in these faces do not know from whom
they are looking. What has to happen has no one
left to happen to. No one is from
anywhere any more. I cannot make it clear.
It is a matter of being. But eyes must be made known."

TO A PLATFORM FULL OF COMMUTERS WAITING FOR THE 9:17 ON WHAT MAY YET BE THE WORLD'S SUNNIEST MORNING

If in fact we are listening
to the same day when we tune
in this morning, will you
tell me, please, what birds
you can be listening to
with any such lack-look in
your eyes, and if no birds,
what *are* all these trees
waving to everywhere we wait?

MISS ASPIC

Sometimes in San Francisco, some
times in Santa Fe, sometimes in
even Newburyport, Massachusetts,
or Jacksonville, or Chicago, or
as if the name of what lies outside what is always the same hotel
could matter, I am in the dim
room with the neon name, virtually
thinking but ritually resisting
the impulse, and in always walks
Miss Aspic, the variously molded
scramble of herself glassily
visible in the gelatinous air
she congeals around her—if
she has one—self, and sits at
the bar, and orders, and opens
her pocket-book, and takes out
her mirror, and does what must be
done till the drink comes, and
takes a sip, and (now) looks more-
or-less around (having memorized
her mirror) and waits and not long.

It is always a long day till time
flies. Miss Aspic is noticeably
for a while some dish. And if she
is not entirely to be looked at too
closely (poor camper on no door-
step), why else are there dim
rooms with neon names? Some sport
will always soon take a flier with
her, and then how the air shakes,

or Miss Aspic's sad jellies, having
forever and forever for a while the
same high time I watch always till
I tire and walk out into the air
and see for myself what same city
it is there all over again always.

IN SOME DOUBT BUT WILLINGLY

Nothing is entirely as one
warbler there in the sun-
hazed tree-top invisibly de-
clares it to be.

What an engine this dawn
has going for it on
that limb I cannot find,
there, or in my mind!

Who wouldn't want to be
that glad, had he the
energy to be reckless about it.
I wouldn't be without it,

were there a choice. I'd
find that limb. I'd hide
invisibly in sun. I'd pump up
light to flood every cup.

I can't make it. I'm too used
to want to. But still bemused.
Go it, bird! Sing! I've had
mornings myself. I'm glad

there are still these
invisible tops to trees
from which a bird can break
a piece of the world awake.

COUNTING ON FLOWERS

Once around a daisy counting
she loves me/she loves me not
and you're left with a golden
button without a petal left to
it. Don't count too much on
what you count on remaining
entirely a flower at the end.

LETTER TO A WRONG CHILD

If ever you need—and who
doesn't?—a mercy not to give
but to take to yourself, a
forgiveness you can live with
outside of those anxiety-
states whose capital Luther
established at Wittenburg hammering
on the door of the church that
had done his forgiving for him—

if ever, that is, you find it
hard to forgive yourself whatever
you did dark in some Keokuk
or Salina or Ashtabula of the
soul. And harder yet to live
unforgiven. And if you lack that
faith whose couch you should have
lain on long since—then, child,
travel.
　　　Go to the oldest cities
and in them avoid tourist-traps.
Make alleys and bad smells your
vocation without sainthood.
Sleep in the beds of the poor.
Peer under the edges of their lives
for dirty leavings. Let them give you
green crusts festively. Take alms
from blind lepers. Study the idioms
of blasphemy, obscenity, and prayer
in all the languages of the hot
countries. If you can beg the

money for it, dial God, and if a
creed answers, hang up.
                              There
will be no need to change your
diet. It will have changed itself. You will, of course, suffer
some malnutrition, but that is
of the prescription.

                    When then you
have grown delirious, when you no
longer know which language you are
not understanding feverishly and
cannot remember exactly which you
arrived with, if any—then
you may present yourself at all
embassies as a distressed national
applying for aid and transpor-
tation. If one of them seems to
understand at least your syntax, you
are probably on your way home.

If possible go by ship. Stand at
the rail in whatever language begins
to return to you and, in it, remember
the old cities—say, Naples, for
instance. You must think of Naples,
however, not as a place but as an
overpopulated idea; as a self-loving,
self-seeking, self-murdering, self-
demonstrating disarrangement and
sequence of ideas made up of too many
other ideas called, sometimes, lives.

Fix your mind on that city-as-idea
(thinking it back to its first blood)
and upon the lives-as-idea moving
through it, and on the sea (of that
rail) moving under it/them.

                 Then if
in seven, ten, twelve, or however many
days that crossing takes, you do not
finally debark free and forgiven and
with a clean, dry, and slightly salty
skin rough to the touch but pleasant
to feel and to be inside of—then,
and only then—it is both permissible
and reasonable to conclude that you are
incurable to your bone and soul, and
to put that bullet, period, through
your otherwise impenetrable head,
my martyr, my poor, alas, white
protestant middle-class wept goose
of this prosperous wrong paved
barnyard.
            With love.
                Father.